Quick&Easy Crochet
Cowls ™

STITCHES 'n STUFF

Contents

POPCORN Cowl

DESIGN BY **FRANCES HUGHES**

SKILL LEVEL

INTERMEDIATE

FINISHED MEASUREMENTS

Approximately 35 inches in circumference x 10 inches wide

MATERIALS

- Sirdar Snuggly Baby Bamboo light (DK) weight bamboo/wool yarn (1¾ oz/104 yds/50g per ball): 4 balls #167 buff brown
- Size H/8/5mm crochet hook or size needed to obtain gauge
- Tapestry needle

GAUGE

3 sc = 1 inch; 2 rows in pattern st = approximately 1 inch

PATTERN NOTES

Join with slip stitch as indicated unless otherwise stated.

Chain-4 at beginning of round counts as a double crochet and chain-1 space.

SPECIAL STITCHES

Beginning V-stitch (beg V-st): Ch 4 (*see Pattern Notes*), dc in indicated st.

Popcorn (pc): 5 dc in indicated st, drop lp from hook, insert hook from front to back in top of first dc, pick up dropped lp and draw through all lps on hook, ch 1 tightly to lock.

V-Stitch (V-st): (Dc, ch 1, dc) in indicated st.

Beginning popcorn (beg pc): Ch 3, 4 dc in same st, drop lp from hook, insert hook from front to back in top of 3rd ch of beg ch-3, pick up dropped lp and draw through all lps on hook, ch 1 tightly to lock.

COWL

Rnd 1: Ch 90, being careful not to twist ch, **join** (*see Pattern Notes*) in first ch to form a ring, ch 1, sc in each ch around, join in beg sc. (*90 sc*)

Rnd 2 (RS): **Beg V-st** (*see Special Stitches*) in same st as joining, dc in each of next 2 sc, **pc** (*see Special Stitches*) in next sc, dc in each of next 2 sc, (**V-st**—*see Special Stitches* in next sc, dc in each of next 2 sc, pc in next sc, dc in each of next 2 sc) around, join in 3rd ch of beg V-st . (*15 V-sts, 15 pc, 60 dc*)

Rnd 3: Sl st in ch-1 sp of beg V-st, **beg pc** (*see Special Stitches*) in same sp, sk next dc of beg V-st, dc in each of next 2 dc, V-st in next pc, dc in each of next 2 dc, (pc in ch-1 sp of next V-st, sk next dc of V-st, dc in each of next 2 dc, V-st in next pc, dc in each of next 2 dc) around, join in beg pc.

Rnds 4–19: [Rep rnds 2 and 3 alternately] 8 times.

BORDER

Rnd 20: Ch 1, sc in same st as beg ch-1, sc in each dc, pc and V-st around, sk ch-1 sps, join in beg sc. Fasten off. (*105 sc*) ∎

COWBOY Cowl

DESIGN BY **SUE CHILDRESS**

SKILL LEVEL

■■□□
EASY

FINISHED MEASUREMENTS

Width at top = 27 inches

Length = 25 inches

MATERIALS

- KFI Luxury Silk light (DK) weight silk yarn (3½ oz/252 yds/100g per hank): 1 hank #8 marigold, violet, sage
- Size J/10/6mm crochet hook or size needed to obtain gauge
- ¾-inch buttons: 5
- Tapestry needle
- Sewing needle
- Matching sewing thread

GAUGE

In pattern: [Tr, ch 1] 7 times = 4 inches; 2 pattern rows = 2 inches

PATTERN NOTES

Chain-5 at beginning of row counts as a treble crochet, and a chain-1 space unless otherwise stated.

Chain-4 at beginning of row counts as a treble crochet unless otherwise stated.

SPECIAL STITCHES

Shell: (Tr, ch 1, tr) in next st or sp.

Beginning shell (beg shell): Ch 5 *(see Pattern Notes)*, tr in indicated st.

Center shell: (2 tr, ch 2, 2 tr) in next st or sp.

Picot: Ch 3, sl st in top of last tr made.

COWL

Row 1: Beg at point, ch 5, **shell** *(see Special Stitches)* in 5th ch from hook (beg sk chs count as a tr), turn. *(1 shell, 1 tr)*

Row 2: **Beg shell** *(see Special Stitches)* in first tr, **center shell** *(see Special Stitches)* in next tr, shell in last tr, turn. *(2 shells, 1 center shell)*

Row 3: Beg shell in first tr, ch 1, tr in next tr, ch 1, center shell in next ch-2 sp, sk 2 tr of center shell, ch 1, tr in next tr, ch 1, shell in last tr, turn. *(2 shells, 1 center shell, 2 tr)*

Row 4: Beg shell in first tr, (ch 1, tr in next tr) across to next ch-2 sp, ch 1, center shell in ch-2 sp, sk 2 tr of center shell, (ch 1, tr in next tr) across to last tr, ch 1, shell in last tr, turn.

Rows 5–19: Rep row 4. *(20 tr on each side of center shell at end of last row)*

Row 20: Ch 4 *(see Pattern Notes)*, sk first ch-1 sp, (center shell in next ch-1 sp, sk next ch-1 sp) across to center shell, center shell in ch-2 sp of center shell, (sk next ch-1 sp, center shell in next ch-1 sp) across to last tr, tr in last tr, turn. *(19 center shells, 2 tr)*

Row 21: Ch 4, tr in ch-2 sp of next center shell, center shell in ch-2 sp of each center shell across to last center shell, tr in ch-2 sp of last center shell, tr in last tr, turn. *(17 center shells, 4 tr)*

Row 22: Ch 4, tr in next tr, tr in ch-2 sp of next center shell, center shell in ch-2 sp of each center shell across to last center shell, tr in ch-2 sp of last center shell, tr in each of last 2 tr, turn. *(15 center shells, 6 tr)*

Row 23: Ch 4, tr in each of next 2 tr, tr in ch-2 sp of next center shell, center shell in ch-2 sp of

Continued on page 14

BOHEMIAN Cowl

DESIGN BY **SUE CHILDRESS**

SKILL LEVEL

■■□□

EASY

FINISHED MEASUREMENTS

33 inches in circumference x 8 inches high

MATERIALS

- Prism Windward medium (worsted) weight rayon/cotton yarn (4 oz/ 200 yds/113g per skein):
  1 skein highlands
- Size G/6/4mm crochet hook or size needed to obtain gauge
- Tapestry needle

GAUGE

2 pattern reps = 4½ inches

PATTERN NOTE

Chain-5 at beginning of row counts as first double crochet and chain-2 space unless otherwise stated.

COWL

Row 1: Ch 34, sc in 2nd ch from hook and in each rem ch across, turn. *(33 sc)*

Row 2: Ch 1, sc in each of first 3 sc, [ch 5, sk next 3 sc, sc in each of next 5 sc] 3 times, ch 5, sk next 3 sc, sc in each of last 3 sc, turn. *(21 sc, 4 ch-5 sps)*

Row 3: Ch 1, sc in each of first 2 sc, [ch 3, sc in next ch-5 sp, ch 3, sk next sc, sc in each of next 3 sc] 4 times, ending last rep with sc in each of last 2 sc, turn. *(17 sc, 8 ch-3 sps)*

Row 4: Ch 1, sc in first sc, [ch 3, sc in next ch-3 sp, sc in next sc, sc in next ch-3 sp, ch 3, sk next sc, sc in next sc] 4 times, turn. *(17 sc, 8 ch-3 sps)*

Row 5: Ch 5 *(see Pattern Note)*, sc in next ch-3 sp, sc in each of next 3 sc, sc in next ch-3 sp, [ch 5, sc in next ch-3 sp, sc in each of next 3 sc, sc in next ch-3 sp] 3 times, ch 2, dc in last sc, turn. *(20 sc, 2 dc)*

Row 6: Ch 1, sc in first dc, ch 3, sk next sc, sc in each of next 3 sc, [ch 3, sc in next ch-5 sp, ch 3, sk next sc, sc in each of next 3 sc] 3 times, ch 3, sc in 3rd ch of beg ch-5, turn. *(17 sc, 8 ch-3 sps)*

Row 7: Ch 1, sc in first sc, sc in next ch-3 sp, ch 3, sk next sc, sc in next sc, [ch 3, sc in next ch-3 sp, sc in next sc, sc in next ch-3 sp, ch 3, sk next sc, sc in next sc] 3 times, ch 3, sc in next ch-3 sp, sc in last sc, turn.

Row 8: Ch 1, sc in each of first 2 sc, [sc in next ch-3 sp, ch 5, sc in next ch-3 sp, sc in each of next 3 sc] 3 times, sc in next ch-3 sp, ch 5, sc in next ch-3 sp, sc in each of last 2 sc, turn. *(21 sc, 4 ch-5 sps)*

Rep rows 3–8 until Cowl measures approximately 36 inches. Fasten off, leaving enough yarn to sew or sl st ends tog. ■

SUMMER SORBET
Cowl
DESIGN BY **SUE CHILDRESS**

SKILL LEVEL

INTERMEDIATE

FINISHED MEASUREMENTS
31½ inches in circumference x 8 inches tall

MATERIALS
- Ella Rae Lace Merino super fine (fingering) weight 100% superwash merino wool (3½ oz/460 yds/100g per hank):
    1 hank #39 melon
- Size E/4/3.5mm crochet hook or size needed to obtain gauge
- Tapestry needle

GAUGE
5 dc = 1 inch; 3 dc rnds = 1 inch

PATTERN NOTES
Join with slip stitch as indicated unless otherwise stated.

Chain-3 at beginning of round counts as a double crochet unless otherwise stated.

SPECIAL STITCH
Cluster (cl): Holding back last lp of each st on hook, 4 dc in indicated st, yo, draw through all 5 lps on hook.

COWL
Rnd 1 (RS): Ch 160, being careful not to twist ch, **join** (see Pattern Notes) in first ch to form a ring, ch 1, sc in same ch, sc in each rem ch around, join in first sc. (160 sc)

Rnd 2: Ch 3 (see Pattern Notes), dc in each of next 4 sc, ch 4, sk next 4 sc, sc in next sc, ch 3, sk next sc, sc in next sc, ch 4, sk next 4 sc, (dc in each of next 5 sc, ch 4, sk next 4 sc, sc in next sc,

ch 3, sk next sc, sc in next sc, ch 4, sk next 4 sc) around, join in top of beg ch-3. (10 pattern reps)

Rnd 3: Ch 3, dc in each of next 4 dc, ch 2, sc in next ch-4 sp, ch 1, 7 dc in next ch-3 sp, ch 1, sc in next ch-4 sp, ch 2, (dc in each of next 5 dc, ch 2, sc in next ch-4 sp, ch 1, 7 dc in next ch-3 sp, ch 1, sc in next ch-4 sp, ch 2) around, join in top of beg ch-3.

Rnd 4: Ch 3, dc in each of next 4 dc, ch 1, **cl** (see Special Stitch) in next dc, [ch 3, sk next dc, cl in next dc] 3 times, ch 1, *dc in each of next 5 dc, ch 1, cl in next dc, [ch 3, sk next dc, cl in next dc] 3 times, ch 1, rep from * around, join in top of beg ch-3.

Rnd 5: Ch 3, dc in each of next 4 dc, ch 2, sc in next ch-3 sp, [ch 3, sc in next ch-3 sp] twice, ch 2, *dc in each of next 5 dc, sc in next ch-3 sp, [ch 3, sc in next ch-3 sp] twice, ch 2, rep from * around, join in top of beg ch-3.

Rnd 6: Ch 3, dc in each of next 4 dc, ch 4, sk next ch-2 sp, sc in next ch-3 sp, ch 3, sc in next ch-3 sp, ch 4, (dc in each of next 5 dc, ch 4, sk next ch-2 sp, sc in next ch-3 sp, ch 3, sc in next ch-3 sp, ch 4) around, join in top of beg ch-3.

Rnds 7–22: [Rep rnds 3–6 consecutively] 4 times.

EDGING
Rnd 1: Sl st in each of next 2 dc, ch 3, 4 hdc in next ch-4 sp, 5 dc in next ch-3 sp, 4 hdc in next ch-4 sp, ch 3, sc in 3rd dc of next 5-dc group, ch 3, (4 hdc in next ch-4 sp, 5 dc in next ch-3 sp, 4 hdc in next ch-4 sp, ch 3, sc in 3rd dc of 5-dc group, ch 3) around, join in base of beg ch-3.

Rnd 2: Ch 3, 5 dc in 2nd hdc of next 4-hdc group, tr in each of next 2 dc, 3 tr in next dc,

Continued on page 14

AZURE SEAS
Cowl

DESIGN BY **SUE CHILDRESS**

SKILL LEVEL

■■□□
EASY

FINISHED MEASUREMENTS

10 inches wide x 28½ inches in circumference

MATERIALS

- Ella Rae Phoenix (worsted) weight 100% Egyptian mercerized Mako cotton yarn (3½ oz/182 yds/100g per skein):
    2 skeins #23 aqua
- Size G/6/4mm crochet hook or size needed to obtain gauge
- Tapestry needle

GAUGE

7 dc = 2 inches; 3 rows in pattern = approximately 2 inches

PATTERN NOTES

Weave in ends as work progresses.

Chain-3 at beginning of row counts as double crochet unless otherwise stated.

Join with slip stitch as indicated unless otherwise stated.

COWL

Row 1: Ch 49, dc in 4th ch from hook (*beg 3 chs count as a dc*), dc in each of next 2 chs, (sk next 3 chs, 3 dc in next ch) 9 times, sk next 3 chs, dc in each of last 4 chs, turn. (*9 3-dc groups, 8 dc*)

Row 2: Ch 3 (*see Pattern Notes*), dc in each of next 3 dc, (3 dc in 2nd dc of next 3-dc group) 3 times, sk last dc of last 3-dc group, dc in each of next 9 dc, (3 dc in 2nd dc of next 3-dc group) 3 times, dc in each of last 3 dc, dc in top of turning ch, turn. (*6 3-dc groups, 17 dc*)

Row 3 (RS): Ch 3, dc in each of next 3 dc, (3 dc in 2nd dc of next 3-dc group) 3 times, (sk next 2 dc, 3 dc in next dc) 6 times, dc in each of last 3 dc, dc in top of turning ch, turn. (*9 3-dc groups, 8 dc*)

Rows 4–49: [Rep rows 2 and 3 alternately] 23 times.

Row 50: Rep row 2.

Row 51: Being careful not to twist piece and with WS tog, hold foundation ch behind last row, working through both thicknesses, sl st in each st across. Do not fasten off.

EDGING

Rnd 1: Turn piece having long edge at top, now working in rnds, with RS facing, working around outer edge, *2 sc around post of turning ch or last dc of each row around, **join** (*see Pattern Notes*) in first sc.

Rnd 2: Ch 1, working left to right, work **reverse sc** (*see Stitch Guide*) in each st around, join in beg reverse sc. Fasten off.

Joining yarn around any turning ch, rep on other outer edge. ■

GOLDEN SPARKLE Cowl

DESIGN BY **SUE CHILDRESS**

SKILL LEVEL

EASY

FINISHED MEASUREMENTS

Top: Approximately 30 inches in circumference

Bottom: Approximately 34 inches in circumference

Length: Approximately 26 inches

MATERIALS

- On Line Bandello medium (worsted) weight cotton/polyamide yarn (1¾ oz/88 yds/50g per skein): 6 skeins #7 taupe
- Size J/10/6mm crochet hook or size needed to obtain gauge
- Tapestry needle

GAUGE

4 hdc = 1 inch; 3 V-st rnds = approximately 2 inches

PATTERN NOTES

Weave in ends as work progresses.

Join with slip stitch as indicated unless otherwise stated.

Chain-2 at beginning of round does not count as a stitch unless otherwise stated.

Chain-5 at beginning of round counts as a double crochet and chain-2 space unless otherwise stated.

Chain-4 at beginning of round counts as a double crochet and chain-1 space unless otherwise stated.

SPECIAL STITCHES

Beginning V-Stitch (beg V-st): Ch 5 (see Pattern Notes), dc in indicated st or sp.

V-Stitch (V-st): (Dc, ch 2, dc) in indicated st or sp.

Beginning decrease V-Stitch (beg dec V-st): Ch 4 (see Pattern Notes), dc in indicated sp.

Decrease V-Stitch (dec V-st): (Dc, ch 1, dc) in indicated sp.

COWL

Rnd 1: Beg at bottom edge, ch 120, being careful not to twist ch, **join** (see Pattern Notes) in first ch to form ring, **ch 2** (see Pattern Notes), hdc in each ch around, join in top of ch-2. (120 hdc)

Rnd 2: Beg V-st (see Special Stitches) in same st, sk next 2 hdc, (**V-st**—see Special Stitches in next hdc, sk next 2 hdc) around, join in 3rd ch of beg ch-5. (40 V-sts)

Rnd 3: Sl st in ch-2 sp of first V-st, beg V-st in same sp, V-st in ch-2 sp of each V-st around, join in 3rd ch of beg ch-5.

Rnds 4–27: Rep rnd 3.

Rnd 28: Sl st in next ch-2 sp, **beg dec V-st** (see Special Stitches) in same sp, **dec V-st** (see Special Stitches) in ch-2 sp of each rem V-st around, join in 3rd ch of beg ch-4. (40 dec V-sts)

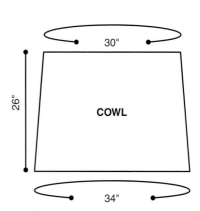

Rnd 29: Sl st in next ch-1 sp, beg dec V-st in same sp, dec V-st in ch-1 sp of each rem dec V-st around, join in 3rd ch of beg ch-4.

Rnds 30–37: Rep rnd 29.

Rnd 38: Sl st in next ch-1 sp, ch 2 *(counts as a hdc)*, hdc in same sp, 2 hdc in ch-1 sp of each dec V-st around, join in 2nd ch of beg ch-2. Fasten off. *(80 hdc)* ∎

COWBOY COWL
Continued from page 5

each center shell across to last center shell, tr in ch-2 sp of last center shell, tr in each of last 3 tr, turn. *(13 center shells, 8 tr)*

Row 24: Ch 4, tr in each of next 3 tr, tr in ch-2 sp of next center shell, center shell in ch-2 sp of each center shell across to last center shell, tr in ch-2 sp of last center shell, tr in each of last 4 tr, turn. *(11 center shells, 10 tr)*

Row 25: Ch 4, tr in each of next 4 tr, center shell in ch-2 sp of each center shell across to last 5 tr, tr in each of last 5 tr, turn.

Rows 26 & 27: Rep row 25. At end of last row, do not turn. Mark for RS.

EDGING
Working down edge of rows, ch 2, 4 hdc around **post** *(see Stitch Guide)* of turning ch, [4 hdc around post of turning ch of next row] 7 times, *sc around turning ch of next row, (3 tr, **picot**– *see Special Stitches*, 3 tr) around post of next row, rep from * 9 times.

POINT
(5 tr, picot) in next row, continue working on other side, 5 tr in next row *(point made)*, **(3 tr,

picot, 3 tr) around post of next row, sc in next row, rep from ** 9 times.

TOP SECTION
4 hdc around post of each of next 7 rows, 6 hdc in last row, working across top, hdc in each tr and each ch-2 sp across, 2 hdc in same turning ch as first hdc, sl st in top of beg ch-2.

BUTTON LOOP ROW
Sc in first hdc, (ch 3, sk next 3 hdc, sc in next 3 hdc) 5 times, sl st in next hdc. Fasten off.

FINISHING
Sew buttons on opposite side of top from Button Loop Row. ∎

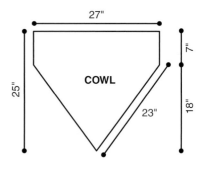

SUMMER SORBET COWL
Continued from page 9

tr in each of next 2 dc, 5 dc in 2nd hdc of next 4-hdc group, ch 3, sc in next sc, (ch 3, 5 dc in 2nd hdc of next 4-hdc group, tr in each of next 2 dc, 3 tr in next dc, tr in each of next 2 dc, 5 dc

in 2nd hdc of next 4-hdc group, ch 3, sc in next sc) around, join in base of beg ch-3. Fasten off and block. ∎

STITCH GUIDE

STITCH ABBREVIATIONS

beg	begin/begins/beginning
bpdc	back post double crochet
bpsc	back post single crochet
bptr	back post treble crochet
CC	contrasting color
ch(s)	chain(s)
ch-	refers to chain or space previously made (i.e., ch-1 space)
ch sp(s)	chain space(s)
cl(s)	cluster(s)
cm	centimeter(s)
dc	double crochet (singular/plural)
dc dec	double crochet 2 or more stitches together, as indicated
dec	decrease/decreases/decreasing
dtr	double treble crochet
ext	extended
fpdc	front post double crochet
fpsc	front post single crochet
fptr	front post treble crochet
g	gram(s)
hdc	half double crochet
hdc dec	half double crochet 2 or more stitches together, as indicated
inc	increase/increases/increasing
lp(s)	loop(s)
MC	main color
mm	millimeter(s)
oz	ounce(s)
pc	popcorn(s)
rem	remain/remains/remaining
rep(s)	repeat(s)
rnd(s)	round(s)
RS	right side
sc	single crochet (singular/plural)
sc dec	single crochet 2 or more stitches together, as indicated
sk	skip/skipped/skipping
sl st(s)	slip stitch(es)
sp(s)	space(s)/spaced
st(s)	stitch(es)
tog	together
tr	treble crochet
trtr	triple treble
WS	wrong side
yd(s)	yard(s)
yo	yarn over

YARN CONVERSION

OUNCES TO GRAMS		GRAMS TO OUNCES	
1	28.4	25	7⁄8
2	56.7	40	1 2⁄3
3	85.0	50	1 3⁄4
4	113.4	100	3 1⁄2

UNITED STATES		UNITED KINGDOM
sl st (slip stitch)	=	sc (single crochet)
sc (single crochet)	=	dc (double crochet)
hdc (half double crochet)	=	htr (half treble crochet)
dc (double crochet)	=	tr (treble crochet)
tr (treble crochet)	=	dtr (double treble crochet)
dtr (double treble crochet)	=	ttr (triple treble crochet)
skip	=	miss

Reverse single crochet (reverse sc): Ch 1, sk first st, working from left to right, insert hook in next st from front to back, draw up lp on hook, yo and draw through both lps on hook.

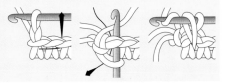

Chain (ch): Yo, pull through lp on hook.

Single crochet (sc): Insert hook in st, yo, pull through st, yo, pull through both lps on hook.

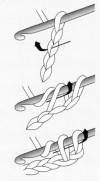

Double crochet (dc): Yo, insert hook in st, yo, pull through st, [yo, pull through 2 lps] twice.

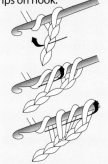

Single crochet decrease (sc dec): (Insert hook, yo, draw lp through) in each of the sts indicated, yo, draw through all lps on hook.

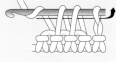

Example of 2-sc dec

Front loop (front lp) Back loop (back lp)

Front Loop   Back Loop

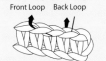

Front post stitch (fp): Back post stitch (bp): When working post st, insert hook from right to left around post of st on previous row.

Back   Front

Post of Stitch

Half double crochet (hdc): Yo, insert hook in st, yo, pull through st, yo, pull through all 3 lps on hook.

Double treble crochet (dtr): Yo 3 times, insert hook in st, yo, pull through st, [yo, pull through 2 lps] 4 times.

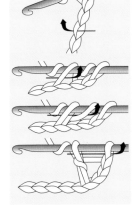

Half double crochet decrease (hdc dec): (Yo, insert hook, yo, draw lp through) in each of the sts indicated, yo, draw through all lps on hook.

Example of 2-hdc dec

Slip stitch (sl st): Insert hook in st, pull through both lps on hook.

Chain color change (ch color change) Yo with new color, draw through last lp on hook.

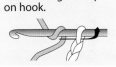

Double crochet color change (dc color change) Drop first color, yo with new color, draw through last 2 lps of st.

Treble crochet (tr): Yo twice, insert hook in st, yo, pull through st, [yo, pull through 2 lps] 3 times.

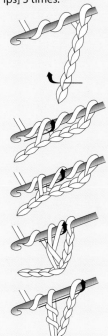

Double crochet decrease (dc dec): (Yo, insert hook, yo, draw lp through, yo, draw through 2 lps on hook) in each of the sts indicated, yo, draw through all lps on hook.

Example of 2-dc dec

Treble crochet decrease (tr dec): Holding back last lp of each st, tr in each of the sts indicated, yo, pull through all lps on hook.

Example of 2-tr dec

METRIC CONVERSION CHARTS

METRIC CONVERSIONS

yards	x	.9144	=	metres (m)
yards	x	91.44	=	centimetres (cm)
inches	x	2.54	=	centimetres (cm)
inches	x	25.40	=	millimetres (mm)
inches	x	.0254	=	metres (m)

centimetres	x	.3937	=	inches
metres	x	1.0936	=	yards

INCHES INTO MILLIMETRES & CENTIMETRES (Rounded off slightly)

inches	mm	cm	inches	cm	inches	cm	inches	cm
1/8	3	0.3	5	12.5	21	53.5	38	96.5
1/4	6	0.6	5 1/2	14	22	56	39	99
3/8	10	1	6	15	23	58.5	40	101.5
1/2	13	1.3	7	18	24	61	41	104
5/8	15	1.5	8	20.5	25	63.5	42	106.5
3/4	20	2	9	23	26	66	43	109
7/8	22	2.2	10	25.5	27	68.5	44	112
1	25	2.5	11	28	28	71	45	114.5
1 1/4	32	3.2	12	30.5	29	73.5	46	117
1 1/2	38	3.8	13	33	30	76	47	119.5
1 3/4	45	4.5	14	35.5	31	79	48	122
2	50	5	15	38	32	81.5	49	124.5
2 1/2	65	6.5	16	40.5	33	84	50	127
3	75	7.5	17	43	34	86.5		
3 1/2	90	9	18	46	35	89		
4	100	10	19	48.5	36	91.5		
4 1/2	115	11.5	20	51	37	94		

KNITTING NEEDLES CONVERSION CHART

Canada/U.S.	0	1	2	3	4	5	6	7	8	9	10	10½	11	13	15
Metric (mm)	2	2¼	2¾	3¼	3½	3¾	4	4½	5	5½	6	6½	8	9	10

CROCHET HOOKS CONVERSION CHART

Canada/U.S.	1/B	2/C	3/D	4/E	5/F	6/G	8/H	9/I	10/J	10½/K	N
Metric (mm)	2.25	2.75	3.25	3.5	3.75	4.25	5	5.5	6	6.5	9.0

Annie's

Quick & Easy Crochet Cowls is published by Annie's, 306 East Parr Road, Berne, IN 46711. Printed in USA. Copyright © 2014 Annie's. All rights reserved. This publication may not be reproduced in part or in whole without written permission from the publisher.

RETAIL STORES: If you would like to carry this pattern book or any other Annie's publication, visit AnniesWSL.com.

Every effort has been made to ensure that the instructions in this pattern book are complete and accurate. We cannot, however, take responsibility for human error, typographical mistakes or variations in individual work. Please visit AnniesCustomerCare.com to check for pattern updates.

ISBN: 978-1-57367-358-7
3 4 5 6 7 8 9